# Go Further with Grammar

EXCLAMATIONS ARE EXPRESSIVE!

ADVERBS ADD EXTRA IMPACT

Ruth Thomson

Thameside Press

US publication copyright © 2002 Thameside Press
International copyright reserved in all countries.
No part of this book may be reproduced in any form
without written permission from the publisher.

Distributed in the United States by
Smart Apple Media
1980 Lookout Drive
North Mankato, MN 56003

Text copyright © Ruth Thomson

**Editors**: Russell McLean, Mary-Jane Wilkins
**Designers**: Rachel Hamdi, Holly Mann
**Illustrators**: Patrice Aggs, Becky Blake, Louise Comfort,
  Serena Feneziani, Charlotte Hard, Brenda Haw,
  Jan McAfferty, Kevin McAleenan, Holly Mann,
  Melanie Mansfield, Colin Payne, Lisa Smith,
  Sara Walker, Gwyneth Williamson
**Educational consultant**: Pie Corbett, Poet and
  Consultant to the National Literacy Strategy

ISBN 1-931983-07-0
Library of Congress Control Number 2002 141337

Printed in Hong Kong

10 9 8 7 6 5 4 3 2 1

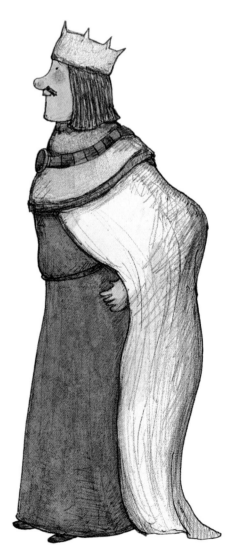

# CONTENTS

# ⭐ USING NOUNS

## What is a noun?

A noun is a naming word for a person, a place, an object, or an animal. Nouns also refer to feelings, such as sadness, and qualities, such as bravery. These nouns always start with a small letter.

a witch

a wolf

a forest

a cup

## List the nouns

 Make a list of the nouns in this writing.

There was so much to do at the theme park. There were dodgems, a tilt-a-whirl, and whirling teacups. There was a scary Ferris wheel, a hair-raising roller coaster, a wild water ride, and a merry-go-round. We wanted to try them all!

## Write a list

Look at these pictures.

 List the fruit in the bowl. List the toys in the basket.

## Proper nouns

Nouns that describe the names of particular people, places, rivers, mountains, countries, days of the week, months, festivals, and the titles of books and films are called **proper nouns**. They always begin with a capital letter.

 Jim Thompson

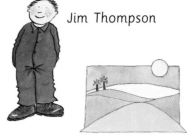 Boston

the Sahara Desert

## Hunt for proper nouns

Find all the proper nouns in this leaflet.

# Stanton Cliff Lighthouse

**Fun for all the family!**

**Opening times**
Easter to October:
Tuesday to Sunday
10A.M.–6P.M.
November to Easter:
Saturday and Sunday
11A.M.–4P.M.

**Admission prices**
Adults                                    $4.50
Children and Seniors        $1.50
Children under 5
and disabled                       FREE

**Refreshments**
The Lookout serves sandwiches, cakes, hot and cold drinks, and ice creams daily, from noon to 4P.M.

**How to get there**
The lighthouse is a five-minute walk from Stanton Station. There is free car and bus parking on the cliff top. The lighthouse is signposted from Ocean Road.

## Make a leaflet

 Write and design your own leaflet for one of these places.

A safari park

 A castle

A nature preserve

A steam-train museum

# SINGULAR AND PLURAL NOUNS

## Making plural nouns

Nouns are either **singular** (only one) or **plural** (more than one). You can turn many singular nouns into plural nouns by adding **-s** or **-es**.

tent
tents

cow
cows

dish
dishes

★ These are some exceptions. Keep a list of any others that you find.

leaf
leaves

goose
geese

man
men

## Hunt for plural nouns

 List all the plural nouns you can find in the writing below.

As the sun set, the pirates slumped contentedly in their chairs. Their cups were empty, their plates were bare, and their tummies were full. The mice feasted on the leftovers, while the gulls hungrily eyed the fishbones. Everyone was feeling sleepy, especially the two children. Cook started clearing the dishes. The only sound was the gentle plop of the fish, dipping and diving in the ocean.

## A wish list

Take turns with a friend to make a wish list using both singular and plural nouns, like this:

I would like a chocolate cake, two kittens, and some football shoes...

...and I would like a new computer and some CDs.

## Collective nouns

Collective nouns describe a group of things.

a **line** of people

a **bunch** of herbs

a **pile** of coins

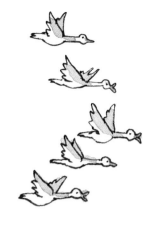

a **flock** of birds

## Hunt for collective nouns

 List all the collective nouns in this piece of writing.

It was payday. The crew waited patiently as Jenny counted out a stack of coins for each of them. A plague of mice squirmed in and out of her chests of treasure.

Meanwhile, Alfie spotted a passing school of fish and tried to catch some for dinner.

A flock of sea gulls flew overhead. Lookout Louis shouted, "Help! Those birds have taken our sack of rice."

## What a lot!

Find or invent some collective nouns to replace the word **lot** in these sentences. Use the picture to help you.

The market was very busy. The vegetable stall displayed **lots** of carrots, **lots** of potatoes, and a **lot** of tomatoes. The fruit stall was piled high with **lots** of grapes and bananas, **lots** of plums, **lots** of apples, and **lots** of oranges. The toy stall was crammed with a **lot** of toys and games, including **lots** of balls, **lots** of beads, and a **lot** of teddy bears.

## Useful collective nouns

| | | | |
|---|---|---|---|
| bunch | bundle | sack | selection |
| set | stack | mound | row |
| clutch | heap | pack | pile |
| string | handful | box | basket |

# NOUN PHRASES

## What is a noun phrase?

A noun phrase is a group of words that does the same work as a noun in a sentence. A noun phrase tells you more about a noun.

✦ You can make a noun phrase by putting an adjective in front of a noun...

**The thin knight** wears green.

✦ Or you can add extra information after the noun...

**The knight with the sharp sword** wears red.

✦ Or you can do both.

**The bravest knight in the world** wears yellow.

### ALIEN ID
Describe these different aliens, using some noun phrases, like this:

**The one-eyed alien with three feet grins with delight.**

## Hunt for noun phrases

 Find the noun phrases in this piece of writing. Make a chart with three columns, labelled **In front**, **After**, and **Both**. Put each noun phrase in the right column.

The noisy procession danced down the narrow street. A swaying girl with a flowery headdress led the way, followed by a dancer in a butterfly costume. A boy in an orange costume blew his shiny trumpet, while the happy boy beside him rattled a tiny tambourine. A masked dancer, a smiling boy wearing a purple hat, and a girl with huge wings bobbed behind them.

# PRONOUNS

## What is a pronoun?

A pronoun stands in place of a noun or a noun phrase, such as:

The cat scratched the velvet curtains. **It** scratched **them**.

The girl with the spotty hat clapped. **She** clapped.

Jane is painting the door. **She** is painting **it**.

The children drank their hot chocolate. **They** drank **theirs**.

## All change

Read the passage below. Decide which nouns you could replace with pronouns to make the sentences read better. Rewrite the text using the right pronouns.

**Alex** was feeling hungry. **Alex** went into **the kitchen**. **The kitchen** smelled of warm **cookies**. **Alex** hoped **Grandma** would give **Alex** a **cookie**, but **Grandma** glared at **Alex** sternly.
"**The cookies** aren't ready," **Grandma** declared. "**The cookies** need to cool."

### Writing tips

✦ Make sure you make it clear who or what each pronoun refers to.

✦ Do not use too many pronouns or you may confuse your readers.

## THINGS TO REMEMBER

• Some pronouns are male or female. They always agree with the nouns that they replace.

**The girl** runs. **She** runs fast.

**The boy** climbs. **He** climbs high.

• Pronouns can be singular or plural. They agree with the noun or nouns they replace.

**Dad** makes a **cake**. **He** makes **it**.

**Birds** eat **worms**. **They** eat **them**.

# USING APOSTROPHES

## What is an apostrophe?

An apostrophe is a punctuation mark. It has two uses.

 You can use it to show that something belongs to somebody.

This is called an apostrophe of possession.

Mom's jeep

my sister's socks

the dogs' bones

 You can also use it to replace one or more letters in a word.

This is called an apostrophe of omission.

I've lost my sock.

I **have** lost my sock.

You'll find it.

You **will** find it.

It's late.

It **is** late.

I can't decide.

I **cannot** decide.

## Add an apostrophe

 Rewrite these phrases, adding an apostrophe in the right place.

Grandmas hat
The ants nest
The gardeners shed
My uncles shirt
The sparrows nest
Annies doll

# What's wrong?

 Rewrite the sentences below, deciding whether or not the word **its** should have an apostrophe.

"What's wrong with this machine?" asked Patsy.

"**Its** not working properly. Perhaps **its** conveyor belt is jammed."

"**Its** all clear inside," replied Oscar.

"Maybe **its** screws need tightening," said Abdul.

"I think **its** blades need sharpening," remarked Mr. Parks.

"**Its** all going to plan," sniggered the spy, peeking at the workers with glee.

# Possession or omission?

Draw two columns and label them **P (for possession)** and **O (for omission)**. Read the text below and write each word with an apostrophe in the right column.

| P (possession) | O (omission) |
|---|---|
| Mr. Wilson's | It's |

**Mr. Wilson's** car was stuck in the muddy field. Its wheels spun round and round, spattering the **boys'** clothes with mud.

"**It's** hopeless," he groaned. "It **won't** budge."

"**Let's** ask the farmer to help us," said Will. "**He's** plowing in the next field."

Following the **tractor's** muddy tracks, the boys waved wildly to attract the **farmer's** attention.

"Our **car's** stuck," they shouted. "Please help us."

Finish the story, using apostrophes in your writing.

# USING ADJECTIVES

## What is an adjective?

An adjective describes somebody or something, such as:

a **huge** fish

 a **square** table

 **pink** ink

 a **furry** koala

 a **friendly** tortoise

💡 **THINGS TO REMEMBER**

To test whether a word is an adjective:

- Does it say more about a noun?
- Can you put it in front of a noun?
  e.g. the **sad** girl
- Can you put it after verbs such as **is, are, feels, looks, gets,** or **seems**?
  e.g. The girl feels **sad**.
  The girl looks **sad**.

## Describe it!

Use adjectives to describe a character, a setting, or the weather. Below are some ideas to start you thinking. List other adjectives you might use for these examples.

**A character**
cruel
snooty
bossy
brave

**A setting**
gloomy
dry
cozy
warm

**The weather**
blustery
thundery
cloudy
rainy

## Boiling or frozen stiff?

These adjectives describe temperatures ranging from incredibly hot to very cold.

white hot
red hot
boiling hot
warm
tepid
lukewarm
chilly
cold
frozen

 Think of adjectives to describe the range between:

- **over the moon** and **heartbroken**;
- **the speed of light** and **a snail's pace**.

## Too many adjectives!

The writing below has too many adjectives. Write your own version. Either choose the most effective adjectives or make some of the nouns more precise.

The happy, cheerful traveler climbed up the steep, sloping, high path towards his home. He had been away for many, countless, numerous years. He was looking forward to sleeping in his own cozy, comfortable, snug bed again.

When he reached the top of the hill, he stopped in complete, utter astonishment. His house was in ruins. Its thick, stone walls were cracked, chipped, and crumbling and there were enormous, gaping holes in the roof.

 Continue the story, using effective adjectives.

## As big as a house

Take turns to imagine something that you have seen. Compare it with something else to create a powerful image, like this:

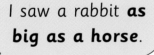 I saw a rabbit **as big as a horse**.

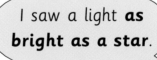 I saw a light **as bright as a star**.

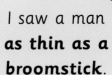 I saw a man **as thin as a broomstick**.

# COMPARATIVES AND SUPERLATIVES

## What is a comparative adjective?

A comparative adjective describes the difference between two things.

Dad is **taller** than Mom.

★ You can make many comparative adjectives from short adjectives by adding **-er** on the end, e.g. kind**er**, tall**er**, clever**er**, dark**er**, loud**er**, rough**er**, old**er**, quiet**er**.

A diamond ring is **more precious** than a gold necklace.

★ To make comparative adjectives of long adjectives (with two or more syllables) add the word **more** to them, e.g. **more** important, **more** beautiful.

## Exaggerate!

You can use comparative adjectives to exaggerate.

It was **colder** than a freezer buried at the South Pole.

He was **hungrier** than a dragon roaring for its dinner.

First think of a comparison, such as:

He is **taller** than a giraffe.

Then exaggerate it:

He is taller than a giraffe **wearing platform shoes**.

## A boastful poem

Write a boastful poem about one of the characters below, using comparisons, e.g.:

Pirate Pete is
Fiercer than a caged tiger,
Stronger than a world
   champion weight-lifter,
Speedier than Superman
   zooming to the rescue.

## What is a superlative adjective?

A superlative adjective describes the person or thing that stands out above all others.

Dad is the **tallest** in our family.

A diamond is the **most precious** jewel.

✦ You can make some superlative adjectives from short adjectives by adding the ending **-est**, e.g. small**est**, old**est**, new**est**, fast**est**, dark**est**.

✦ To make other superlative adjectives, put **most** in front of the adjective, e.g. **most** important, **most** interesting, **most** beautiful.

## Hunt for superlatives

 List the superlative adjectives in the writing below.

Only the bravest knights sat down to eat. The smallest, hungriest knight was thrilled that he had as much to eat as the tallest one. The fattest knight had the smallest plate with the least food and was the most unhappy. The thinnest knight had the biggest plate and the most food. He was the happiest of them all!

## It's the best!

Advertisements often use superlatives to persuade people to buy something or to go to a particular place or event.

Runaway roller coaster

Come for a ride on the longest, scariest, most amazing, most unforgettable ride ever!

 Design and write an advert for one of these, using some superlative adjectives.

A tricycle

A pop CD

An ocean resort

A camera

# ✩ USING VERBS

## What is a verb tense?

A verb is the word that tells you what is happening in a sentence. The tense of the verb tells you **when** something happens.

✴ The **present** tense tells you that an event is happening now.

✴ The **past** tense tells you that an event has already happened.

✴ The **future** tense tells you that an event will happen in the future.

The boy **blows up** a balloon.

The diver **landed** on the seabed.

**I will see** a kangaroo when I go to the zoo.

 Today, last week, or next week?

Think of a sentence. Take turns to change it, beginning with **Today**, **Last week**, or **Next week**. Make sure you use the same verb and the correct verb tense each time.

THINGS TO REMEMBER

- To discover whether a word is a verb, see whether you can change its tense.
- Some verbs in the past tense end in **-ed**, such as look**ed**, liv**ed**, explain**ed**.
- One way of making the future tense is to put **will** or **shall** in front of the verb. e.g. I **will** go. I **shall** sing.

**Today,** I am **writing** my diary.

**Last week,** I **wrote** a story about a shark.

**Next week,** I **will write** about my trip to England.

# Present, past, or future?

Read these sentences. There is a description, a forecast, some instructions, and a story. Which is which? What tense are they in?

On Sunday, it will rain throughout the country. By Monday, the skies will clear and the weather should be sunny.

White Castle stands on top of Banner Hill. From the main tower, there are great views over the countryside.

To avoid mosquito bites, use an insect-repelling cream and keep your skin covered at night.

David peeped into the garden and gasped. A pair of sheep in shirts and shorts were twirling to the music from his radio.

Write your own weather forecast, a description of a famous building, and instructions for using suncream.

# A complete change

The past tense of many verbs is completely different from the present tense. There is something wrong with the verbs in the writing below.

 List the correct past tense for each verb.

Jan waked up and finded someone had bringed him an apple. He taked a big bite and beginned to feel very light. Soon he flyed up in the air and goed higher and higher. He thinked it ised fun until the wind blowed him out to sea and the spell weared off. He falled into the water. Luckily, a fisherman seed him and comed to rescue him.

## Writing tip

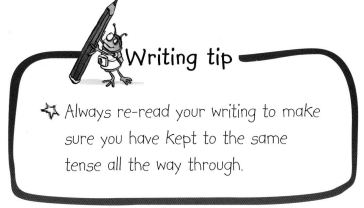

✦ Always re-read your writing to make sure you have kept to the same tense all the way through.

# POWERFUL VERBS

## Give it some power!

A powerful verb can describe a person's character or mood or suggest the atmosphere of a place.

Spot the powerful verbs below. What atmosphere do they suggest?

What was that noise? The children crept out of bed and tip-toed downstairs. They paused outside the kitchen door and heard the strange sound again. Their hearts raced as they inched open the door and peeked into the room.

Continue the story, using verbs which create the same atmosphere and feelings.

### Powerful verbs

| | | | |
|---|---|---|---|
| peered | wailed | whispered | murmured |
| glimpsed | whimpered | sneaked | squirmed |
| squealed | pattered | rustled | fled |
| swished | shrieked | slumped | flopped |

## Happy, sad, or grumpy?

What do the verbs in these sentences tell you about how each child is feeling?

Maria **stamped** into the classroom.
Josh **sidled** into the classroom.
Annie **bounced** into the classroom.
Imran **mooched** into the classroom.
Billy **skipped** into the classroom.

Write another sentence that tells you more about each person's mood, such as:

Maria stamped into the classroom. She banged down her bag, crossed her arms, and scowled.

## Ate, said, and went

List some more powerful verbs that also mean **ate**, **said**, or **went**. Try them in the sentences below.

Bobby **ate** his sandwich.

Jerry **went** up the hill.

Mom **said**, "Look at this."

## What's up?

Choose one of these characters and give him or her a name. What sort of person is he or she? What has just happened? How is the character feeling? What will he or she do next?

 Write an account, using powerful verbs to describe how the character feels.

 Writing tips

★ Describe characters by the way they move, eat, talk, react, or look at something.

★ Use a thesaurus to help you find different powerful verbs.

## Change the verbs

 Rewrite this text, replacing the dull verbs with powerful ones.

Jamie **went** down the lane. He **went** into a field and **put** his bike against a tree. He **put** his picnic on a blanket. Then he **put** his hands in the stream. When he **went** back, he **saw** three geese **standing** near his food.

Bees were **going** over the fruit bowl.

Jamie **put up** his hands and **said**, "**Go** away!"

# ☆ USING ADVERBS

## What is an adverb?

An adverb gives extra meaning to a verb or a sentence. An adverb can tell the reader:

**How?**
He swims **strongly**.

**Where?**
He swims **away**.

**When?**
He swims **today**.

✦ Many adverbs are made by adding **-ly** to an adjective, e.g. bad**ly**, slow**ly**, soft**ly**, strange**ly**.

✦ The adverbs **very**, **quite**, **really**, **more**, **most,** and **as much as** can say more about an adjective.

I'm **quite** tired.

I'm **very** happy.

I'm **really** angry.

## PLAY THE GAME When, where, and how?

Imagine there has been a robbery. Take turns to describe when, where, and how it happened, using an adverb in your answer.

It happened **yesterday**.

It took place **outside**.

The robber drove away **speedily**.

## What a difference!

An adverb can change the meaning of a sentence. Try finishing the sentence below with each different adverb. See how each adverb alters the meaning.

The robot waited...

calmly

defiantly

anxiously

quietly

impatiently

miserably

cheerfully

 Write down some alternative adverbs for these two sentences.

The friends whispered **excitedly**.

He **hurriedly** set off.

## Hunt for adverbs

Find the adverbs in this passage.

Gradually, the rain stopped. The wind blew gently through the trees and drops of water fell softly onto the soggy ground. Slowly, the animals came out of hiding. The monkey swung swiftly from tree to tree in search of fruit.

A frog beadily eyed the mosquitoes swarming noisily in the hot sunshine.

A colorful parrot watched the two explorers tie up their boat carefully.

 Write your own description of a rain forest, using some interesting adverbs.

## All quiet?

Make this text more exciting by replacing **quietly** with alternative adverbs.

**Quietly**, the explorers landed on a grassy bank. Jane peered **quietly** at some footprints, while Leo **quietly** watched a monkey. Neither of them noticed the jaguar stalking **quietly** along a branch, nor the alligator **quietly** swimming towards them.

 Writing tip

⭐ Try to vary the position of adverbs to make sentences more interesting.

**Sadly**, she looked at her brother.

She looked **sadly** at her brother.

She looked at her brother **sadly**.

21

# How do they do it?

Pick one of the characters below. Then choose one of the actions (verbs) from the purple box, and one of the adverbs from the blue box. Finally, write down your sentence.

e.g. **Grandma dances badly.**

| verbs | adverbs |
|---|---|
| dances | slowly |
| splashes | loudly |
| eats | badly |
| jumps | grumpily |
| calls | fast |
| pounces | gracefully |
| plays | lazily |
| behaves | happily |
| creeps | wearily |
| sings | well |
| smiles | naughtily |
| stamps | silently |

The nurse    The sailor    Grandma    The skeleton    The girl

The cat    The mouse    The bird    The frog    The monkey

# Speak up!

When you write a conversation, use adverbs to show how characters speak. Find the adverbs in the conversation below. Find the powerful verbs as well.

"Look at that octopus!" shouted the captain fearfully.

"It's MASSIVE!" exclaimed one of the crew.

Jenny asked anxiously, "Could it climb aboard?"

"I doubt it," said One-eyed Jim, reassuringly.

"It's coming closer," shrieked Aunt Alice.

"It looks very angry," Pirate Pete said grimly.

 Continue the pirates' conversation, using suitable adverbs to show how they speak.

 Writing tip

✿ Do not use too many adverbs. Sometimes it is more effective to use a powerful verb instead.

# WRITING SENTENCES

## What is a sentence?
A sentence makes sense. The simplest sentence has a **subject** and a **verb**.

| The boy | sits. |
|---------|-------|
| (subject) | (verb) |

A simple sentence has a **subject**, a **verb** and an **object**.

| The boy | strokes | the cat. |
|---------|---------|----------|
| (subject) | (verb) | (object) |

 **THINGS TO REMEMBER**

- The verb ending changes according to the subject.

| I play. | He plays. | We play. |
|---------|-----------|----------|
| I am. | She is. | We are. |

## Make some sentences

 Take each **subject** in turn. Write a sentence, choosing a **verb** and an **object** that makes sense.

| Subject | Verb |
|---------|------|
| I | plays |
| You | make |
| He | mends |
| She | see |
| We | cut |
| They | breaks |
| My friend | eats |
| His mom | cleans |
| | finds |
| | wears |

### Object

fire

jewelry

present

star

ball

cake

recorder

fish tank

mask

car

sweater

stew

dishes

jeans

sandcastle

 **Writing tips**

When you write sentences:

✰ Always start with a capital letter and end with a full stop.

✰ Check that the verb ending agrees with the subject.

23

# USING COMMAS

## What are commas for?

✦ Commas help show where extra information has been added to a sentence.

Jack, **my brother**, plays with his cat.

or

Jack plays with his cat, **Spot**.

✦ Commas can also separate a list of actions. They show where there are breaks in the meaning of a sentence.

The bell rang for lunch. The children stopped work, washed their hands, sat down at the table, and waited for their food.

## Add the commas

 Write some funny sentences, using the names, characters, and actions below.

e.g. **Leo, a shaggy dog, is learning to fly.**

Make sure you use commas to mark the extra information about the character.

| names | characters | endings |
|---|---|---|
| Mr. Potter, | a brilliant drummer, | eats too fast. |
| Paul, | the clumsy clown, | talks nonsense. |
| Amrita, | your crazy friend, | cycles to work. |
| Leo, | a shaggy dog, | is learning to fly. |
| Annie, | our long-lost uncle, | wears silly hats. |
| Mrs. Muffet, | my baby sister, | annoys me. |

## Take action!

Choose one of these sentences.

- Lightning streaked across the night sky.
- There was a knock at the door.
- There was a groan from under the bed.

Write a second sentence that follows on from it. Pick up clues about the setting from the first sentence. Include a list of actions, using commas to separate them, like this:

**Lightning streaked across the night sky.**
The clashing knights cut short their midnight duel, opened their visors, shuddered with alarm, and dropped their swords.

# CHANGING SENTENCES

## How long is a sentence?

A sentence can be as short or as long as you like.

> The mermaid sang.

or The mermaid sang to the fish under the sea.

★ You can add words (nouns, adjectives, and adverbs):

> **Alice**, the **happy** mermaid, sang **beautifully** to the fish under the sea.

★ You can change words:

> The mermaid **hummed**.

★ You can extend a sentence:

> The mermaid sang to the fish under the sea **because she was feeling so happy**.

★ You can re-order the words:

> Beautifully, the mermaid sang to the fish.

## Play with sentences

Pick one of these short sentences and change it in as many different ways as you can. Use the pictures to help you.

- Add adjectives, adverbs, and phrases.
- Change words, using precise nouns and powerful verbs.
- Extend the sentence.
- Change the order of the words.

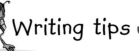

My grandma looked up.

The children hid.

The door opened.

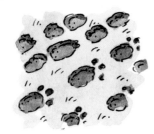

I found footprints.

### Writing tips

Make sentences interesting by extending them, re-ordering the words, or changing or adding words.

Think carefully where to put adverbs. Compare the impact of **suddenly** in these two sentences:

**Suddenly**, he stopped.

He stopped **suddenly**.

# QUESTIONS AND EXCLAMATIONS

## What types of sentences are there?

**Statements**
The wolves howled at the moon.

**Questions**
When is your birthday?

Could you talk more quietly please?

**Exclamations**

I don't believe it!

**Instructions**
Pull the ends tight.

## Asking questions

Change each statement below into a question. With some of them, you can re-order the same words. With others, you will need to change the verbs.

Mom had been reading the newspaper.

They were sledding in the park.

She could be washing her hands.

The baby is shaking her rattle.

Bob can play the trombone.

Stars twinkle at night.

The sun will be shining soon.

### Writing tips

✦ Use questions to talk to and engage your readers,

e.g. Feeling hungry?
What was that?

✦ Remember to put a question mark at the end of a question.

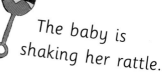

Joe might be painting the fence.

Jason made a toy theater.

## What is an exclamation?

✦ Exclamations make your readers pay attention. They may order, bully, or surprise.

The verb is often at the beginning.

**Run faster!**     **Buy now!**
**Help!**          **Hurry up!**

✦ Exclamations show strong feelings, such as joy, wonder, pain, anger, or surprise.

**Ouch!**          **That's fantastic!**
**Wow!**           **Go away!**

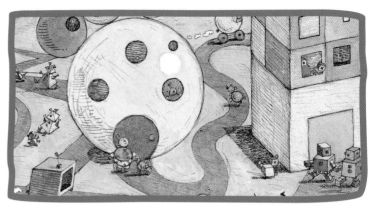

✦ They may not always include a verb.

**What an amazing place!**

✦ Exclamations always end with an exclamation point.

## Buy now!

Advertisements often use questions, statements, instructions, and exclamations to encourage you to buy something.

Is your backyard swing comfortable?

Snuggle and snooze all day long

in our stylish and superior SOFA SWINGER.

Buy now while stocks last!

Do you long to keep cool on hot, summer days?

Our ever popular PLISH-PLASH WADING POOL is the answer.

Don't miss this special summer offer!

Write an advertisement of your own. Include at least one question, one statement, and one instruction.

# USING CONNECTIVES

## What are connectives?

Connectives are linking words.

 Some connectives can be put in the middle of sentences to join two ideas. These are called **conjunctions**.

The words **and**, **because**, **so**, **or**, **but** are conjunctions.

Joe threw the Frisbee **and** James caught it.

Other connectives come at the beginning of sentences. They link ideas between two separate sentences.

Joe hit the ball. **However,** no one could catch it.

## Choose a conjunction

Take turns to make a sentence longer using different conjunctions.

I ran all the way **but** the shop had closed.

I ran all the way **because** I was late.

I ran all the way **although** I was tired.

## Join two sentences

How many different ways can you link these pairs of sentences? Choose some connectives from the box below.

The tractor stopped.
The farmer jumped out.

Jim played the guitar quietly.
Grandma woke up.

Ella saved her pocket money.
She bought a watch.

They put up the tent.
It started to rain.

### Useful connectives

| | | | |
|---|---|---|---|
| and | after | also | because |
| before | but | finally | first |
| besides | later | next | in the end |
| or | when | while | then |
| although | as | if | until |

## For or against

Some connectives are useful for presenting an argument.

### Is exercise necessary?

| For | Against |
|---|---|
| **Many people believe** that exercise keeps you healthy. | **On the other hand**, exercise can be hard work. |
| **One reason** is that your heart pumps much harder during exercise. | **Some people say** exercise is boring. |
| **Another reason** is that you use all your muscles and keep them in good shape. | **Besides**, people need a good space and proper equipment. |
| **Furthermore**, exercise makes you feel good. | **In addition**, people may do too much exercise and exhaust themselves. |
| **Also**, you can exercise with your friends. | **Furthermore**, they may injure themselves. |
| **Finally**, exercise can be fun. | **Finally**, it takes a huge effort to keep exercising regularly. |

In conclusion, I think that exercise is a good idea because it keeps people healthy and happy.

Choose one of these questions. Make a **for** and **against** chart like the one above. Write arguments for both sides, using connectives to help structure your reasons.

- Should we dump garbage at sea?
- Should children watch as much TV as they like?
- Should cars be banned from downtown centers?

# Writing checklist

After you finish your first draft, read it through carefully.
Check the following points before you write the final draft.

## ✦ Sentences

- Does every sentence have a verb?
- Are the sentences different lengths? Are any too long?
- Do the sentences start in different ways?
- Are they interesting?
- In conversations, does each new speaker start on a separate line?

## ✦ Verbs

- Are all the verbs in the same tense?
- Are they powerful?
- Do the verbs agree with the nouns?

## ✦ Nouns

- Do proper nouns start with a capital letter?
- Have you used some pronouns, so that nouns are not repeated too often?
- Are the nouns precise?

## ✦ Adjectives

- Does every adjective add new information?
- Could you use a precise noun instead?

## ✦ Adverbs

- Have you used adverbs to help describe some of the verbs?
- Are they in the most effective place? Try moving them around in your sentences.

## ✦ Punctuation

- Check whether you have used the correct punctuation. Read your draft aloud to hear how it sounds. See whether the punctuation will make readers pause where you want them to.

## ✦ Powerful writing

Can you improve your writing to make it more powerful and expressive?

- Trim some of the sentences to make them more dramatic or to speed up the action.
- Extend other sentences to describe or explain something more fully.
- Use some questions and exclamations to draw readers in and to add suspense or surprise.
- Add some adjectives, noun phrases, and adverbs for extra color.
- Re-order some of the sentences to add interest.

# Glossary

**adjective**

An adjective tells you more about a noun.

The **tall** boy caught a **huge** fish.

A **comparative adjective** describes the difference between two things.

Dad is **taller** than Mom.

A **superlative adjective** describes the person or thing that stands out above all others.

Dad is the **tallest** in our family.

**adverb**

An adverb gives extra meaning to a verb, an adjective, or a sentence.

The robot waited **miserably**.

**apostrophe (')**

An apostrophe is a punctuation mark.
An **apostrophe of possession** shows that something belongs to someone.

My sister**'**s socks.

An **apostrophe of omission** replaces two or more letters in a word.

I**'**ve lost my sock. (I **have** lost my sock).

**comma (,)**

A comma is a punctuation mark. It tells the reader when to pause. Commas separate things in a list or any extra information in a sentence.

Jack**,** my brother**,** plays with his cat.

**connective**

A connective is a linking word in the middle of a sentence or between two sentences.

I ran all the way **because** I was late.

**exclamation**

An exclamation shows a strong feeling or gives an order. It ends with an exclamation point (**!**).

"**Come here!**" shouted Ben.

**noun**

A noun names a person, a thing, a place, a quality, or a feeling.

a **witch**, a **cup**, a **forest**, **bravery**

A **collective noun** refers to a group.

a **pile** of coins

A **proper noun** names a particular person, place, day of the week, month, festival, or organization. It starts with a capital letter.

**Paris**, **Monday**, **Easter**, the **Red Cross**

**pronoun**

A pronoun takes the place of a noun.

Alex is hungry. **He** eats a cookie.

**question**

A question is a sentence that asks something. It ends with a question mark (**?**).

**When is your birthday?**

**sentence**

A sentence describes an event or a situation. It has a subject and a verb and makes sense. It starts with a capital letter and ends with a full stop, a question mark, or an exclamation point.

**The boy strokes the cat.**

**verb**

A verb is the word that describes what is happening in a sentence.

Maria **stamped** into the classroom.

**verb tense**

The verb tense tells you when something happens either now (in the present), in the past, or in the future.

He watch**es**.    (present)
He watch**ed**.    (past)
He **will** watch. (future)

# Index

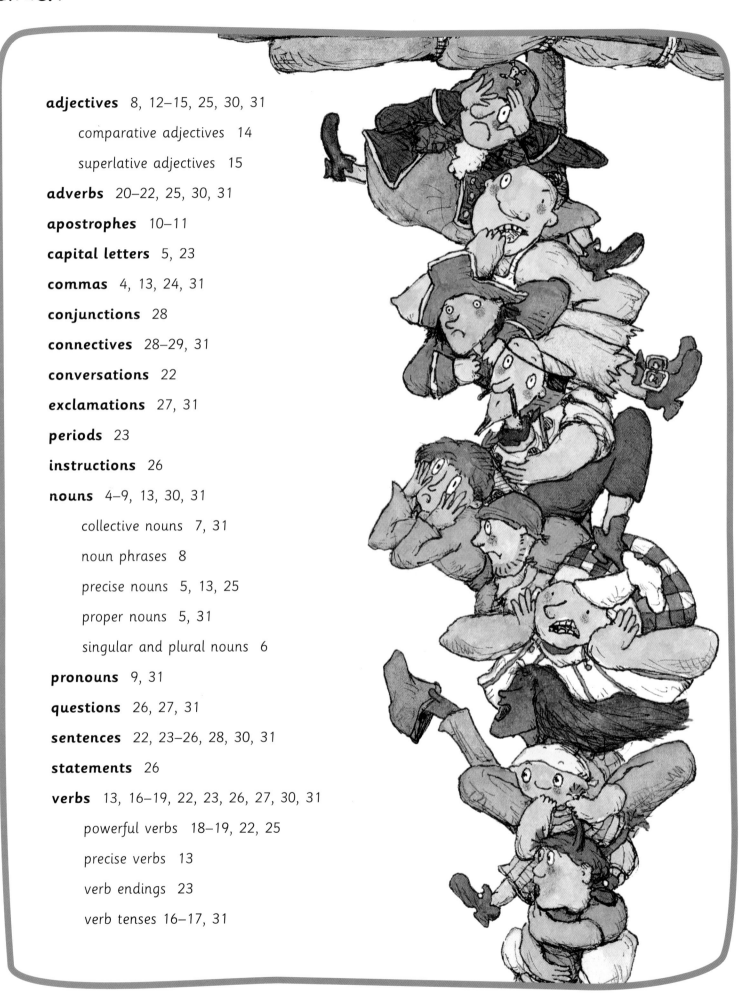